Simple

Muffins

Steven Stellingwerf

ILLUSTRATED BY GAIL ROTH

KEY PORTER BOOKS

First Published in 1992 by
The Appletree Press, Ltd
19–21 Alfred Street, Belfast BT2 8DL

Published in Canada by:

Key Porter Books Ltd
70 The Esplanade
Toronto, Ontario
Canada M5E 1R2

Canadian Cataloguing in Publication Data

Stellingwerf, Steven
Perfectly simple muffins

ISBN: 1-55013-421-3

1. Muffins I. Title.
TX770.M83S74 1992 641.8'15 C92-094519-8

Printed in the E.C.

92 93 94 95 96 5 4 3 2 1

Introduction

I hope this little book of muffin recipes will show you just how simple muffins are to prepare. Indeed, muffin recipes do not require fancy ingredients or complex preparation to make the result taste good.

Tradition has it that muffins were first baked as a breakfast bread and they are still considered a breakfast pastry worldwide. Through the years, the tradition has changed slightly, and muffins are now considered appropriate fare for any time of the day, breakfast being the most popular, then lunch and afternoon tea, and even those special holiday feasts with family.

This book is divided into the four seasons of the year, with suggestions for muffins suitable for a particular month, depending upon holidays and the availability of fruit.

A note on measures

For all recipes in this book, muffin tins should be filled $^2/_3$ full of batter. Spoon measurements are level except where otherwise indicated.

Christmas Muffins

With the rich, candied fruit-and-sherry taste of these muffins, they're sure to whet hungry appetites on a cold winter morning. They can be served warm or at room temperature and will complement any Christmas brunch menu.

1/2 cup sherry
1/3 cup raisins
1/4 cup candied pineapple, finely chopped
1/4 cup candied cherries
1/4 cup slivered almonds
2 cups flour
2 tsp baking powder
1 tsp salt
1/2 tsp allspice
1/2 tsp ground cinnamon
1/2 cup sugar
1 egg
1/3 cup butter, melted
1 cup milk

(makes 12)

Preheat oven to 350°F. Soak fruit in sherry overnight in a covered container. In a medium bowl combine flour, baking powder, salt, allspice, cinnamon, and sugar until well blended. Add egg, butter, and milk. Stir together until well blended. Fold in fruit and nuts until just mixed. Bake for 20 minutes.

Apple Streusel Muffins

This recipe was shared with me by a very good friend who has been in the catering business for several years. It is one of the most requested muffins that she bakes.

2 cups all-purpose flour
1 cup sugar
1 tbsp baking powder
1 1/4 tsp cinnamon
1 cup apples, finely chopped
1/2 tsp baking soda
2 eggs
1 cup sour cream
1/4 cup butter, melted
1/2 tsp salt

Streusel Topping

1/4 cup sugar
3 tbsp flour
1/2 tsp cinnamon
2 tbsp butter

(makes 18 muffins)

Preheat oven to 350°F. In a large bowl stir together flour, sugar, baking powder, cinnamon, salt, and baking soda. Set aside. In a small bowl, beat eggs, sour cream, and butter. Add all at once to dry ingredients. Fold in apples, stirring only until slightly blended. Sprinkle topping on muffins and bake for 25–30 minutes.

Hot Cross Muffins

A tasty substitute to serve your guests on Easter morning instead of traditional hot cross buns. Also considered a sweet bread, these muffins blend in well with any Easter meal, whether it be a sunrise brunch or the traditional dinner feast.

2 cups all-purpose flour
1 tbsp baking powder
1/2 tsp salt
2 tsp cinnamon
1/2 tsp nutmeg
1/2 cup sugar
1 egg
1/3 cup butter, melted
1 cup milk
1 cup mixed candied fruit, chopped

Icing

1 cup confectioner's sugar
2 tbsp milk
1 tbsp melted butter
1/2 tsp vanilla extract

(makes 12)

Preheat oven to 350°F. Sift flour, baking powder, salt, cinnamon, nutmeg, and sugar together. Stir egg, butter, and milk into flour mixture until slightly blended. Fold in candied fruit until mixed. Bake for approximately 20 minutes, or until lightly browned. Cool. Beat

Gingerbread
Muffins

confectioner's sugar, milk, butter, and vanilla extract until well blended, about 3–5 minutes. Pipe a cross on the top of each muffin.

Gingerbread Muffins

Gingerbread Muffins are at their best when served at room temperature. This gives the many spices in the recipe time to reach their full flavor.

$^{1}/_{4}$ cup butter, at room temperature
$^{1}/_{4}$ cup molasses
1 egg
1$^{1}/_{3}$ cups all-purpose flour
$^{1}/_{2}$ tsp salt
$^{1}/_{2}$ tsp baking powder
$^{1}/_{2}$ tsp soda
2 tsp cinnamon
1 tsp ground ginger
$^{1}/_{2}$ tsp ground cloves
$^{1}/_{2}$ cup hot water
1 cup raisins
(makes 20–24)

Preheat oven to 350°F. Blend butter and sugar until light and fluffy. Beat in molasses and egg. Add dry ingredients to creamed mixture alternately with hot water until well blended. Fold in raisins. Bake for approximately 15 minutes or until muffins are golden brown.

Refreshing Lemon Muffins

These muffins are bursting with the refreshing flavor of lemon and make a light snack when served with afternoon tea. They will also complement a bowl of fresh fruit nicely.

2 cups all-purpose flour
1 tbsp baking powder
1 tsp salt
1/2 cup sugar
1 egg
1 cup milk
1/3 cup butter, melted
2 tbsp lemon peel, grated
2 tsp lemon extract
1/2 cup pecans, chopped
(makes 18)

Preheat oven to 350°F. Sieve together flour, baking powder, salt, and sugar in a small mixing bowl. Add egg, milk, and butter, stirring until well blended. Fold in lemon peel, lemon extract, and pecans so that the batter is slightly mixed. Bake for 20–25 minutes.

Orange Poppy Seed Muffins

Normally served by themselves, Orange Poppy Seed Muffins are easily adapted. They taste wonderful when cut in half, spread with butter, and filled with thinly sliced ham.

1 cup sugar
1/3 cup butter, at room temperature
1 egg
1 tbsp poppy seeds
1/2 tsp soda
2 tbsp orange peel, grated
2 tbsp orange juice
1/2 cup sour cream
1 1/3 cups all-purpose flour
1/2 tsp salt
(makes 12)

Preheat oven to 350°F. Mix the sugar, sour cream, butter, and egg thoroughly. Stir in poppy seeds, baking soda, orange peel, orange juice, flour, and salt until slightly blended. Bake for 15–20 minutes or until lightly browned.

Morning Glory Muffins

With its mélange of ingredients and moist texture, this muffin has grown to be one of the most popular baked today. It is so popular, indeed, that some say the Blueberry Muffin has taken second place now to the Morning Glory Muffin.

2 cups all-purpose flour
1 1/4 cups white sugar
2 tsp baking soda
2 tsp cinnamon
1/2 tsp salt
2 cups carrots, grated
1/2 cup raisins
1/2 cup walnuts, chopped
1/2 cup shredded coconut
1/2 cup grated apple
3 eggs
1 cup vegetable cooking oil
3 tsp vanilla extract
(makes 24)

Preheat oven to 350°F. In a large bowl combine flour, sugar, baking soda, cinnamon, and salt. Stir in carrots, raisins, walnuts, coconut, and apple. In a bowl, beat eggs, oil, and vanilla extract until well blended. Stir into flour mixture until batter is just slightly combined. Bake for 20 minutes. Do not overbake.

FLOUR

Honey Bran Muffins

So moist, delicious and full of flavor are these muffins that you would never know they are a healthy way to start off the morning.

1 cup pineapple, crushed and undrained
1 1/2 cups wheat-bran cereal
2/3 cup buttermilk
1 egg
1/3 cup pecans, chopped
3 tbsp vegetable oil
1/2 cup honey
2/3 cup whole-wheat flour
1/2 tsp baking soda
1/2 tsp salt
(makes 12)

Preheat oven to 350°F. In a large mixing bowl combine pineapple, bran cereal, and buttermilk. Let this stand until cereal has soaked up the liquid. Stir in eggs, nuts, oil, and 1/3 cup of the honey. In a small bowl mix flour, baking soda, and salt. Stir into bran mixture until slightly blended. Bake for approximately 15–20 minutes when muffins should be golden brown.

Ginger Pear Muffins

With their spicy flavor and moist texture, these muffins are bound to be a success. Not only can they be eaten with a main meal but, sliced in half with a scoop of ice cream in the center, they create a wonderfully refreshing dessert.

2 cups all-purpose flour
$^{3}/_{4}$ cup brown sugar, firmly packed
1 tsp baking soda
1 tsp salt
2 tsp ground ginger
1 tsp ground cinnamon
$^{1}/_{2}$ tsp ground cloves
1 cup plain yogurt
$^{1}/_{2}$ cup vegetable cooking oil
4 tbsp molasses
1 egg
2 cups pears, diced
$^{1}/_{3}$ cup walnuts, chopped
(makes 18)

Preheat oven to 350°F. In a large bowl mix flour, brown sugar, baking soda, salt, ginger, cinnamon, and cloves until thoroughly mixed. In a separate bowl, mix yogurt, oil, molasses, and egg until well blended. Combine yogurt mixture to flour mixture and blend slightly. Fold in pears and walnuts. Bake for 25 minutes.

Blueberry Muffins

I can remember being served a warm blueberry muffin with a hot bowl of chilli on cold weather days by my mother. I also remember the story of how her mother served the same meal to her when she was little. Now grown, I still enjoy these muffins with any meal.

3 cups all-purpose flour
1 tbsp baking powder
1/2 tsp baking soda
3/4 cup sugar
1 1/2 tsp salt
2 cups blueberries
2 eggs
3/4 cup milk
1/2 cup butter, melted
1 tbsp orange peel, grated
1/2 cup orange juice
1 1/2 tbsp lemon juice
(makes 24)

Preheat oven to 400°F. Sift flour, baking powder, baking soda, sugar, and salt into a bowl. Add blueberries and roll until coated with flour. In a large mixing bowl, mix eggs, milk, butter, orange peel, orange juice, and lemon juice. Add the flour and blueberry mixture and stir until blended. Bake for 20 minutes.

Zucchini Muffins

A few years ago my grandmother shared this recipe with me as one she had discovered and considered to be very good. Once I had tried it, I had to agree. It is a very moist and tasty muffin and one sure to remain a favorite with successive generations.

3 eggs
3 tsp vanilla extract
3 tsp ground cinnamon
1/2 tsp ground nutmeg
3 cups all-purpose flour
1 cup vegetable oil
2 cups zucchini, grated
2 cups sugar
1 tsp baking soda
1 tsp salt
1 tsp baking powder
(makes 24)

Preheat oven to 350°F. Mix together eggs and vanilla extract, beat until well blended. Add cinnamon, nutmeg, flour, oil, and zucchini to egg mixture and blend well. Continue to add sugar, baking soda, salt, and baking powder and blend well. Bake for 15–20 minutes.

Cinnamon

Cranberry Muffins

With its sweet flavor and tart aftertaste, this muffin makes a wonderful afternoon-tea sandwich when cut in half and filled with thinly sliced turkey. The muffins can be baked in a large muffin tin for regular-size sandwiches, or in a mini-muffin tin for tea sandwiches.

1 1/2 cups all-purpose flour
1/2 cup sugar
1 tsp baking powder
1/2 tsp baking soda
1/2 tsp salt
2 eggs
1/4 cup butter, melted
1/2 cup sour cream
1 tsp almond extract
1 cup fresh or frozen cranberries or 1/3 cup whole-berry cranberry sauce

(makes 8–12)

Preheat oven to 350°F. Mix together flour, sugar, baking powder, baking soda, and salt in a large bowl. In another bowl blend eggs, butter, sour cream, and almond extract. Pour egg mixture over flour mixture and mix slightly until just blended. Fold in cranberries until just mixed. Bake muffins for approximately 25–30 minutes.

Peanut Butter Muffins

This is a favorite among children because of its outstanding peanut-butter flavor. Sliced in half and spread with jam, this muffin tastes like a peanut-butter-and-jam sandwich.

1 cup bran cereal flakes, crushed
$1\frac{1}{2}$ cups all-purpose flour
1 tsp salt
$1\frac{1}{2}$ cups milk
4 tbsp butter, melted
5 tbsp brown sugar
3 tsp baking powder
2 eggs
$\frac{2}{3}$ cup peanut butter, crunchy
(makes 18)

Preheat oven to 400°F. In a bowl mix together the branflakes, flour, salt, brown sugar, and baking powder. In another bowl mix the peanut butter and milk until smooth. Add the eggs and melted butter. Beat well. Combine this with the dry ingredients. Bake for 15–20 minutes or until golden brown.

1 CUP

Banana Muffins

This recipe goes back several generations as a banana loaf bread, passed on to me by my grandmother. To this day she still uses this recipe on special occasions. Its unique ingredient is the maraschino cherries which enhance the rich flavor of the bread. I choose to adapt it by baking the recipe in muffin tins instead of loaf pans, which works perfectly.

1 cup sugar
1/2 cup butter
2 eggs
1 cup mashed ripe bananas
2 cups all-purpose flour
1 tsp baking soda
1/2 tsp salt
1/2 cup pecans, chopped
1/2 cups maraschino cherries, chopped
(makes 12)

Preheat oven to 350°F. In a bowl cream sugar, butter, and eggs until light and fluffy. Add bananas and beat so that the batter is well mixed. Add flour, baking soda, salt, pecans, and maraschino cherries and mix once again until well blended. Bake for approximately 20 minutes or until muffins are golden brown.

Surprise Jam Muffins

Just as their name suggests, everyone who bites into these muffins will get a surprise. The centers can be filled with all sorts of jams and jellies depending upon the baker's preference.

1 3/4 cups all-purpose flour
1/4 cup sugar
2 1/2 tsp baking powder
3/4 tsp salt
1 egg
3/4 cup milk
1/3 cup cooking oil
jelly or jam
(makes 18)

Preheat oven to 400°F. Mix flour, sugar, baking powder, and salt. Beat the egg and add milk and oil to the beaten egg. Pour milk mixture over flour mixture. Stir until all the flour is wet and well blended. Fill greased muffin pans 1/3 full. Add 1 teaspoon of jam or jelly and then fill pans with more batter so that they are 2/3 full. Bake for 20 minutes.

Chocolate Chip Muffins

Any chocoholic is bound to love this muffin and its many chocolate chips. Whether you are a chocolate fan or not, you will soon taste how wonderful chocolate can be in muffins.

2 cups all-purpose flour
1 tbsp baking powder
1 tsp salt
$^{1}/_{2}$ cup sugar
$^{1}/_{3}$ cup brown sugar
1 egg
$^{1}/_{2}$ cup butter, melted
$^{1}/_{2}$ cup milk
$^{1}/_{2}$ cup sour cream
$1^{3}/_{4}$ cups chocolate chips
1 cup walnuts, chopped
(makes 12)

Preheat oven to 350°F. In a medium bowl combine flour, baking powder, salt, and sugars. In another bowl blend egg, butter, milk, and sour cream until well blended. Add flour mixture to butter mixture and mix well. Fold in chocolate chips and walnuts. Bake muffins for approximately 15–20 minutes.

Date Muffins

Dates, the main ingredient in these muffins, are readily available all year round as are pecans, so this is not a seasonal muffin. Appropriate for any time of the year, these muffins freeze well.

1 tbsp butter
1 tsp baking soda
1 cup boiling water
1 cup dates, chopped
1/2 cup pecans, chopped
1 cup sugar
1 egg yolk
1 3/4 cups all-purpose flour
1 tbsp vanilla extract
1 tsp salt
(makes 18)

Preheat oven to 325°F. Put butter and baking soda in a small bowl and add the cup of boiling water. Place dates and pecans in a small bowl and pour boiling-water mixture over them. Cool for approximately 30 minutes. Mix in sugar, egg yolk, flour, vanilla extract, and salt. Bake for approximately 20–25 minutes.

SUGAR

Orange Date Muffins

Combine two of the best flavors available, and you'll create a muffin that is hard to resist.

2 cups all-purpose flour
1 tbsp baking powder
1 tsp salt
3/4 cup sugar
1 egg
1/2 cup butter at room temperature
1 cup milk
grated peel from 1 orange
1/3 cup orange juice
1 cup dates, chopped
1 cup walnuts, chopped
(makes 12)

Preheat oven to 350°F. Combine flour, baking powder, salt, and sugar in a small bowl. In another bowl slightly blend egg, butter, and milk. Add flour mixture, blending until just mixed. Fold in orange peel, orange juice, dates, and walnuts. Bake for approximately 20 minutes.

Strawberry Muffins

When your markets are full of ripe red strawberries, you'll want to try this recipe. Fresh strawberries are the key to the moist flavor of these muffins.

1 1/2 cups 100% bran cereal flakes
1 1/2 cups milk
1/2 cup whole-wheat flour
1 tbsp baking powder
1 tsp salt
3/4 cup brown sugar, firmly packed
1 egg
1/3 cup butter, melted
1 1/2 cups finely chopped fresh strawberries,
(makes 12)

Preheat oven to 350°F. Pour milk over bran flakes and let soak for 20 minutes. Sift together flour, baking powder, salt, and brown sugar. Add to bran-flake mixture. Blend well. Stir in egg and butter to flour mixture until just blended. Gently fold in finely chopped strawberries. Bake for approximately 20 minutes.

Pumpkin Muffins

When the leaves turn their autumn colors, a chill is in the air, and Hallowe'en is just around the corner, it's the perfect time to try these pumpkin muffins.

3 cups sugar
1 cup cooking oil
4 eggs
1½ tsp salt
1 tsp cinnamon
⅔ cup water
2 cups pumpkin, cooked (or canned)
3½ cups all-purpose flour
½ tsp ground ginger
½ tsp ground cloves
2 tsp baking soda
1½ tsp vanilla extract
2 cups chopped walnuts
(makes 30)

Preheat oven to 350°F. In a large mixing bowl combine sugar, oil, eggs, salt, cinnamon, water, and pumpkin until well blended. Add remaining ingredients and blend well so that batter is mixed thoroughly. Bake for 15–20 minutes.

Cherry Nut Muffins

This is a simple recipe to prepare and bake and proves that muffins do not have to be difficult to prepare to taste good.

2 cups all-purpose flour
1 tsp baking powder
1 tsp salt
1 cup sugar
1 egg
1/3 cup butter
1 cup milk
1 cup pecans, chopped
1 cup maraschino cherries, chopped
(makes 18)

Preheat oven to 350°F. In a medium bowl combine flour, baking powder, salt, and sugar. Mix until well blended. Add egg, butter, and milk and stir until just mixed together. Fold in pecans and cherries. Bake for approximately 20 minutes.

Brand

Rhubarb Muffins

This is considered a summer muffin because rhubarb is so plentiful during the summer season. If you plan in advance, though, you can chop and freeze the rhubarb ahead of time, then use it all year round. Rhubarb muffins have an enjoyable and unique taste that you can only fully appreciate when you bite into one.

$1\frac{1}{4}$ cups brown sugar, firmly packed
1 egg
$\frac{1}{2}$ cup vegetable oil
2 tsp vanilla extract
1 cup buttermilk
$1\frac{1}{2}$ cups rhubarb, diced
$2\frac{1}{2}$ cups all-purpose flour
1 tsp baking soda
1 tsp baking powder
$\frac{1}{2}$ tsp salt

Topping

1 tbsp butter, melted
$\frac{1}{3}$ cup sugar
2 tsp cinnamon

(makes 20)

Preheat oven to 400°F. In a bowl, combine the brown sugar, egg, oil, vanilla extract, and buttermilk, mixing until well blended. Add the rhubarb and fold in by mixing. In a separate bowl, stir together the flour, baking soda, baking powder, and salt. Add the dry ingredients to the rhubarb batter. Stir until just blended. Sprinkle each muffin with the butter, sugar, and cinnamon topping. Bake for 20–25 minutes.

Maple Muffins

As maple syrup was first developed in the southern United States, these have always been considered traditional southern muffins. Through the years, they have worked their way north via friends and relatives and are now enjoyed throughout America.

2 cups all-purpose flour
1 tbsp baking powder
1/2 tsp salt
1/4 cup sugar
1 egg
1 cup milk
1/2 cup butter
2/3 cup maple syrup
2 tsp maple extract
1 cup walnuts, chopped
(makes 12–18)

Preheat oven to 350°F. In a small bowl mix flour, baking powder, salt, and sugar. Add egg, milk, butter, maple syrup, and maple extract and blend until well mixed. Fold in walnuts until slightly blended. Bake for approximately 20–25 minutes.

Maple Muffins

Pineapple
Oatmeal Muffins

Pineapple Oatmeal Muffins

These two unique ingredients complement each other so well that you will be amazed at how moist and delicious these muffins are. I know this recipe will be considered one of your favorites.

1/2 cup vegetable oil
1/4 cup orange juice
2 eggs
1/2 cup brown sugar, firmly packed
2 tsp grated orange rind
1 1/2 cups rolled oats
1 cup crushed pineapple, with juice
1 1/2 cups all-purpose flour
1 tbsp baking powder
1 tsp baking soda
1 tsp salt
(makes 18)

Preheat oven to 350°F. In a large mixing bowl combine oil, orange juice, eggs, brown sugar, and orange rind. Mix until well blended. Fold in oats and pineapple. Add flour, baking powder, baking soda, and salt. Mix together and blend well. Bake for 20–25 minutes.

Raspberry Muffins

These muffins have always been one of my favorites, and their refreshing raspberry taste will be difficult to resist.

2 cups all-purpose flour
1 tsp salt
1 tbsp baking powder
2/3 cup sugar
1 egg
1/2 cup milk
1 tsp vanilla extract
1/3 cup butter, melted
1/2 cup sour cream
2 cups raspberries
(makes 12)

Preheat oven to 350°F. Stir together flour, salt, baking powder, and sugar. Blend in egg, butter, milk, sour cream, and vanilla extract. Gently fold in raspberries. Bake for 20 minutes.

Peach Muffins

Peach muffins are easy to prepare and are very economical; with the versatility of using canned peaches instead of seasonal fresh peaches, the cost remains low and the muffins can be made year round.

1/2 cup butter at room temperature
3/4 cup sugar
1 egg
1 1/2 cups all-purpose flour
2 tsp baking powder
2 tsp vanilla extract
1/2 tsp salt
1/2 cup plain yogurt
1 cup chopped canned peaches, well drained
1 cup chopped pecans
(makes 15)

Preheat oven to 350°F. Cream butter and sugar until fluffy. Add egg and beat well. Beat in vanilla extract and yogurt. Stir in flour, baking powder, and salt. Add peaches and pecans until just blended. Bake for 20 minutes or until lightly browned.

Black Cherry Muffins

The distinctive flavor of these muffins makes them a great favorite. They are best when served cooled and spread with whipped butter and are a refreshing delight with any spring morning brunch.

2 cups all-purpose flour
1 tbsp baking powder
1/2 tsp salt
1/2 cup butter at room temperature
2/3 cup sugar
2 eggs
2 tsp vanilla extract
1/2 cup milk
1 1/2 cups pitted black cherries, chopped
(makes 12)

Preheat oven to 350°F. In a medium bowl mix flour, baking powder, and salt. Dust 1 tablespoon of the flour mixture into the cherries. Cream butter and sugar until light and fluffy. Add egg and vanilla extract and continue to beat for 3 more minutes. Blend in flour mixture alternately with milk. Fold in cherries until just slightly mixed. Bake for 25 minutes.

Sweet Potato Muffins

Though similar to the Pumpkin Muffin, the Sweet Potato Muffin has a unique and subdued flavor of its own. This moist muffin is delicious when served as a bread with any main meal.

1/2 cup butter
1 1/4 cups sugar
2 eggs
1 1/4 cups mashed sweet potatoes (yams)
1 1/2 cups all-purpose flour
2 tsp baking powder
1/2 tsp salt
1 tsp cinnamon
1 tsp nutmeg
1 cup milk
1/2 cup pecans, chopped
1/2 cup raisins
(makes 24)

Preheat oven to 350°F. Cream butter and sugar until light and fluffy. Add eggs and mix well. Blend in sweet potatoes. Add dry ingredients and spices alternately with the milk and mix slightly. Fold in pecans and raisins. Bake for 25 minutes.

Index